THE ODES TO TL61P
of
KESTON SUTHERLAND

THE ODES TO TL61P
of
KESTON SUTHERLAND

ENITHARMON PRESS

First published in 2013
by Enitharmon Press
26B Caversham Road
London NW5 2DU

www.enitharmon.co.uk

Distributed in the UK by
Central Books
99 Wallis Road
London E9 5LN

Distributed in the USA and Canada
by Dufour Editions Inc.
PO Box 7, Chester Springs
PA 19425, USA

ISBN: 978-1-907587-27-6

Enitharmon Press gratefully acknowledges the financial support of
Arts Council England through Grants for the Arts.

British Library Cataloguing-in-Publication Data.
A catalogue record for this book is available
from the British Library.

Printed in England by SRP

And the situation is like that in certain games, in which all places on the board are supposed to be filled in accordance with certain rules, where at the end, blocked by certain spaces, you will be forced to leave more places empty than you could have or wanted to, unless you used some trick. There is, however, a certain procedure through which one can most easily fill the board.

Wake up my fellow citizens and middle class and go look into the mirror.

ODE TO TL61P 1

1.1

Each time you unscrew the head the truths burn out
and fly away above the stack of basements inundated
in aboriginal mucus, elevating the impeccable,
hereafter congenitally depilated Janine rescaled to a
grainy blank up on to the oblong top of the freezer
whose shut white lid unhinged at the back alone
preserves a pyramid of rigid meat, budget pizzas,
devirginated arctic rolls, only ever kidding in a
prophylactic void torn into great crates of glittering
eye shadow, dousing all its stickiness in dark empty
swerves, for no-one is the radius of everything we
are, a reinforced steel artery in the very integument
to be burst asunder, by reason of innately shattered
strobes as soon lived as burnt out, ramming an unplanned
crack into the door mechanism; who the fuck I am
now speaking to or at or for or not at this moment
is compensation for being completed into a circle
resigned to resume the first square, the first on the
entire board, and is listening there, afloat and spent yet
lost in streaks to the opening night whose primitively
explosive starlight is progressively nit-picked from a
lately impatient and fidgeting sky, not far too far or fast
too inquisitively squinted at, its cartilage of crudely
lubed-up open access sex arcs scraped out piecemeal
and in single file, and once there inaudibly ask yourself
why; inside it is the fundamental sky of shining fact:
the abolition of capital *is* the social revolution: state

again this single fact, in too deep for any scar; in the end, which is right now, *looming* over a motto executed in the Ottoman style of the rococo circumlocution in liberal sex jargon recited by Ériphile at II.i.477-508, in the dreamiest mannequins' subsequent scan of which smudged erotic jottings allege to a scratched-out holographic ear the improbable lovable double-stranded far end of the primitive primary streak canal bound in stratified squamous epithelium to an alternatively screaming mouth, destined while dying inside to repeat before dying outside one last infinity of one-liners before snapping and giving up, or better yet pretending to, once you get it, once that is you really get it all, or not at all, directly into the hot squamocolumnar junction with its intestate teat cistern, a photocopy blurred into alienating aleatory *poésie concrète* by being roughly swiped back and forth over the scratched platen glass of the Canon MF8180C or Brother DCP-9045CDN all-in-one fax, printer and copier of the redacted catechism that stubs out the abrupt Shelley's 'Triumph of Life', later pruned to talking points, under the table propped up at right angles folded until they froth, to triple its unaccountability to an afflatus, doing as the banks just did not as the banks just said, I understand the hole that George is in, a dot whose innuendo comes too late, flush with spirit toilet-trained to life, but sucking on the aging raging hard-on held in trust for young dysphagia who only comes of age, yes exactly but at the same time, or at some other time like it, or at what is not a time but is still like it, if not exactly like it, or at what is exactly not a time and therefore not exactly like it, or not like this, or in an unsustainable combination of the above, to be waked to death and faked alive, for the known good of bored stiff rich men whose sexuality is literalised into a rampage of leverage and default swaps, hovering above minimum wage like a bloodthirsty erection over a fairground mirror, inspected from on icy high with seething and with licking, to want to absolutely spit it out, whose incessant re-entry is a background music *still* more popular than real because forever liable to be rewound, rammed again and again into the gaping ingrown unclipped ears of outgrown human sex toys gated off, ground down, caved in and blown up to do anything you can think you will do and then do what you think or fear you will do and then do as you fear you are told or would rather not do but nonetheless do or only die wishing you had already done or never had, grinding a fickle reality out, a kind of backlit soft porn nativity scene constructed out of versican, fudge icing and nail clippers, *shhh*, to prove the point of passion is immutable as fire strips (This is conducive to heat and does not require frequent cleaning, saving time and effort and money. Second, the pipe is a sheet metal processing products, the advantages of uniform thickness is unparalleled) or inimitable for money right up to the two-speed marital Martin Amis, repel all thought, one-speed once you know the ropes of growing insensitive, gaining the hill, from which a further speed is deducted for every emergent callous, until at the crux, when finally you give up ramming it because it has no point, it has minus a trillion preset speeds, shoots a mawkish moreish seed, basting shit and sugar-coating nil, whose real name is a liberal anagram for amniotic trim, not for TL61P or the reverse on principle to which the self-same letters cling in blanket terror of being peeled off by a rigid sexy acrylic fingernail later filed to oblivion through the eye of whose cameo done in grisly nitrocellulose and gritty ochre/lavender of your mother in the late style of the perpetually born yesterday Francis Bacon dissembling his tantrum to dead meat bunged in oil in an overhead Tefal Maxifry inanely overheated to open the end up half empty of Fair and Lovely a single, infinitesimal, silver plated, tiny ring slowly and invisibly spins, summoning in all the cast the obligation to remain within it, latterly as a cortège, our magic antennae screwed to our antic macramé, an opening in the opening night, savaged by the light it marginalises; but before anyone could actually get hard or wet or both at once for leading members of that cast, lead role models for our past, who beg to differ, slave to eat *the mess we inherited from the last* orgasm in government for sexy workers whipped to slurp the surplus spew of petty change remaindered when the banks have had their due, their in any case very eccentric final countdown redacted to a catchphrase for obsolescence per pro oral compliance with the takeover speculation boosting Autonomy Corp. 5.3% after better than estimated earnings forecasts at Oracle Corp., our flat back teeth drilled in the new international tax regime protologisms, refuting enamel, chipping in to Tesco, scorning accessibility, adrift in gum, virtual for real, adages on bandages, paper cuts in water damage, implants of the daily grind, children out the almost real and almost shut but not decisively shut yet and still shatterproof smeary and eternally not real window sing *the mess we inherited from the last* beginning scraps the missing past to recycle the joy it brings, the power set, of a subset, of a power set, of a sex power,

suburbanites of backstreet Überbollywood in flower
for the first time since you not only die
at all since how could you not; biting
starts too late, sucking is original,
is already there, free with age;
grab a plastic sheet full of milk to toss out the shut
door and catch it. TL61P infix and
feed the flame its sparks, to burn how it matters,
strict instruction voided blank
to prime the end for drying to a glare, bright
rivets on the profound water,
and under the water, the reason it's there.
von Feuer der Arbeit beleckt, to come
a random liquid tripwire, a head's tuft's caressed ash,
knotted to Iraqi satisfaction; by the fire
of labour, dead debt rips out prank alien loins,
this way up, to any moon you like;
the back of your first lover pressed in your groin.

   But if that will keep its grip
in there since not exhausted from
   without a light dissolves to rip
and shine again was all I am,
   plating the air humans exhale
in that window I flex in dark;

   to take the point not ready yet
to give you back but adamant
   by idiotic mantras to earn
the reason for love's apparent
   deterrence so long after you
my blood races I can't pull out;

you that will not come back led
in there to have the life you get
    too close; to be the slanting bed
too far away to make you up
    or lose you in; go under me
and stare at the same thing apart.

*

Our glaring end annuls in light
    what fire on the faded past
remains whose shadow cannot last
    as you burn away in bright

and widespread too ecstatic loss
    everywhere bends the eye
back on the slow infinity
    that blocks the love it fits across

just as rehoused at random love
    itself puts up its opposites
cut down to make the point it is
    not wasted in the end to prove.

In Mexico the problem has another dimension, owing
to the drug cartels and the human cost of their
iconicity, much of it dialectical and in women. There
they throw sackfulls of decapitated heads all over
the disco floor; just skidding on it like a male child
is naïve, but kicking them around is, if anything,
worse: at that point *everything* is deeply interfused,
even the congealed, invisible, virtual, abstract, spectral,
projected white blood cells rushing barely at trace
levels to the head of the slowest nail ever hammered

in Ichkeria into a pineapple, a wrist, silence, or into
the base of the hammer itself, a pat plastic simile for
a slapdash splintering spine, thinking cheap as dirt
and free as verse; Prometheus was a misogynist; its
testimony is the unbearable faintness of its odour in
your heart, this blood that is beginning everywhere;
but the present catastrophe (ll.485-6) rebrands Félix
Gallardo as the primary object, locked-up ladder
to its elite sublimities, so that strutting in golden
ringlets streaked with ashen highlights on the sexual
proscenium at the
boundary of significance we may know him, his too hot crotch
in knots of living weasel gut, whispering only just to love,
If it's not interesting to read then what's the point in doing it
or living as though you have to, defined by an obligation with
no fulfilment, lapsing to prognosis of a soap aisle?
I start my investigation here, taking my life in my hand.
Life rises to greet me, boasting its ardency in the carotid.

1.2

dusters wrapt in itching flame, streaked in limbic cloud
pt in itching *l* 6
blue sky on the setting water, nod til
made to still, remade in onward chains?
T
Looking out the plane window at the feather grass and spiders,
the three p bears
a triangle dunked in the oil prism a head left.
Who knows if what I'm thinking is this, or worse?
Dispersing the riot in smoke like love in conscience:
"the use value of a thing does not concern its seller as
such, but only its buyer." In which case use values are

exclusive to consumers, and consumers are in that case the Blinky, Pinky, Inky and Clyde of the way of despair squared, so that as our art is increasingly sold, and love is, and there are many more sellers, many of them good sellers, its use value as what the Nigerians call a supernumerary proportion of its total combined value including its exchange goes into improbable dramatic decline, like Chekhov. We *feel* this as consumers, not as one, readying ourselves not to, and are forever almost ready; staring at the alien in the thousand eyes it blinks, making up for consciousness with all the shit it thinks. Move your arms around, doing work. Click to the melody under your nails. Nothing changes this into a specimen of forever, very quickly, but quiet as impatience spreads down the shoulder into the thin end of the teeth the wind will brush the edge like water cracked apart, exposure for exhibitionist brains, plated with very heaven. AWM6140/3, allegations, water on the genitals, sisters in photographs, belt-tightening, electric dreams, speak in starts distractedly. The game has no ending – as long as the player keeps at least one life, he or she should be able to continue playing indefinitely. This is rendered impossible by a bug. You task Madiha Shenshel with cooking your breakfast (hawk eggs in fried milk, high in polycollaterals), then finishing it, then making it again (fuck, a dot), automatically spitting shells out; you prefer the boxes to the toys; Deborah's photo of herself crammed into her college wardrobe, ad infinitum; the hair on a thousand mothers; infinity ad nauseam; the internal level counter is stored in a single byte, and when it reaches 255 the subroutine causes this value to roll over to zero before drawing the fruit. This causes the routine to draw 256 fruits, or wish to, which corrupts the bottom half of the screen and the whole right half of the maze with seemingly random symbols, making it unwinnable. But reality is not at the bottom of the abyss, the abyss is in time just reality being itself, at least to begin with and at the same time conclusively as if contracted – *soft* – to a single point (a dot) at the end of the universe, when dark matter is a distant memory subject for chastisement to the fluctuations of military nostalgia (in her foot), and I am not sure to go on, or how to, or even what name that is any more, whoever you are I do *this* for, person *this*, human *this*, *this* window for *this* crack, or even if I do it, and probably I don't, the strings on a thousand dolls, relief at Abu

Naji I cite its adaptation on bliss in memory,

retread via Danny Boy to the drool igloo, pseudo-TL61P

atom jus, disqualified for living

cleared – the fruits and intermissions would restart the anaemia fade *this* the possibility *this* the price of bread in 1792 *this* Mariana asleep in bed in a beansprout bound in spattered marble, staring at the skin next to your eye

free of that universe, mimetic of a smudged cherry

Traherne: love is deeper than at first it can be

thought, and the extra will last you

past care to a better joke about

you drilled through to infiltrate the gothic froth of Helmand.

1.3

But really to believe that necessity is exhausted, if it comes, making haste to apologise for its premature infantilism by a great, clumsy show of increase in salivation flow, once best left alone not otherwise, by

going on longer, the point itself will still be around, is
a *joke*: embryo smut in the possible taste. Since once
you get from A to B, take your time returning. Isn't
it the problem that I *want* you to stare at me until
our eyes trade sockets, trailing visions, fucking our
mutual brains out all over the wrongest floor, not the
implication that hooding was banned in 1972 that asks
for an adaptation on bliss in memory? Light
sockets, the halo pinned to bodies in remorse,
devoured in a shadow life sends back?
Remember this: I sort through the boxes,
my first poems are there, the
drawings I made at school are
and my toys are, lead prodigies and barbarians,
Paints for them, tapes of my rock band
some vinyl of Tchaikovsky and Bach, the present
photographs of my first sexual lover,
whose face is staring with intent euphoria
and deepening tenderness at the face I
was, the eyes I shone in then, the light
in them blinds me now to nothing less
than under your caress I can do still,
and do still even right now, or very soon do
when I climb into bed with you and let
my arm shrink into your waking head,
or sleeping, however you are in there,
that room of objects and that room of you.

II

Construction may routinely be upgraded into life
as orphic vanity spreads backwards
its only motive for the present obscurity.

But deafness has an adverse impact on
interrogation, smiling at the lips in oil
for food is fast by proxy to an epic patronage
I want, take, scream, stick

• •

You try to replenish the sounds that you hear
in your head, regimental amnesia –
I saw all the members of the multiple emulate me
unfold into an illicit epigram I now laterally hyperventilate,
one line with a joke end at the end
backing inspiration, breathing parerga of children and plangent dill;
ties it together, asks? *The Retracting,*
acting like ears, downed in void; a fur
of fire on *lick*
me you on this line when you don't
expect it when you do, this line.
It has a rim you take out to the bottom of the floor
big enough to remand your first genitals;
the rim is rectangular as any Seurat, to forever ruin
the way you wait, I'll be here forever.
A winding sheet of shining eyes, slammed to annihilation.

III

Nothing
we did could get him to open
the door the roof was coming down he's
driving us somewhere but where the
light fits like a door kicked in
the head on a shoestring right to do
its worst and make the best of you,
at the back to be alone
so that in the wet graphics spraying out the

spoils of the grave a dead friend in
shreds gladly climbs and with
growling stomach and powdered flower
roots to snort in dust steps on
the podium of odium to trill this elegy:
I have a dream of every man I ate in
all my life, / and after that
refreshment no zombie can pick his teeth,
/ but better learn to live with
what he's got and what he's not, /
and make both tolerances perfectible.
There's no way in as you defer to that,
this way back from rejecting it to see;
repeat yourself after me: repeat it
yourself after me: repeat yourself at me: I am
at alone in all the world a mirror
forfeit to beauty: the love I am is anything
what I live for, skin and looking at
you dead now but like at your breath still
sharp at the flesh of desiring we ran
out from, liquid across the floor
they tore down years ago, live in your hand
my face, a stick of empty fingertips.
The code TL61P belongs to a Hotpoint dryer.
You'll find out nothing if you look
it up through the sky in the screen, the vault
of exchangeable passion, Vertigo at
the horizon prostrate as an outstretched
cheek; but in the mouth that grows
in capacity behind that overflow,
Nobody can take away the word for it:
love, the provisional end until death;
TL61P its unconditional perfected shadow
opposite; Now go back to the start.

ODE TO TL61P 2

I

What the public hears from the police on TV is the voice of police management. Everyone who has a manager knows what that litotic brachylogy always sounds like. You learn in the end to pick out the buzzwords like hairs from a dessert you only think you don't want to eat now, whereas in truth it is what you have paid for in order that you can be too intimidated to complain about it or send it back, by way of sending yourself back instead, and though the mouthfeel is like a grease-filled crack except astonishingly ugly you study to roll your eyes, pucker as if embittered, and furtively smirk at the gelatine soufflé with the other patriotic bulimics. When during the live BBC News 24 footage of the clearance of Trafalgar Square on the 26th March 2011 the police "commander" (think of your area manager going by that name) explained for the benefit of sedulous licensees who own the perk of Freeview that the people presently adopted under the state truncheons are not protesters but criminals intent on chaos, not one because they cannot be but the other because they are, what he *meant* was 1. The plan to camp out in Trafalgar Square is tactically brilliant and must not succeed; real passion really does make disproportionate analogies powerful; the disproportion of Trafalgar to Tahrir would be no disincentive to solidarity; it would also appeal too much to overexercised Arabs, here and in the region; it would give Al-Jazeera an unwelcome brief commercial edge against Sky. 2. When the rank and file are angry and bored of tolerating teenage insubordination, you toss them some roughage of which they may boast that they feel entitled to it "after a tiring day"; you watch them get their revenge, you get an anal-sadistic bliss kick out of watching them do it only because you allow them to; they will think you are turning a blind eye to their excesses and be very flattered (this is what management *always* thinks). 3. It was late at night and the police in the square were being paid overtime; the bit of extra cash for its members would slow the impetus of the police union, which would be a welcome window of opportunity for the managers paid fortunes which are however already diminishing because of high inflation to dilate on our frontline cuts, in any case in spite of the rampant inflation of everything that is, owing to whatever is now the meaning for avarice, of which fit readers will be pleased to remember that Athenaeus colourfully remarked in his *Deipnosophistae* that it hopes to drag Pluto out of the bowels of the earth; 4. The windows at Millbank are not yet fixed. You are strangulatingly disentangled from the tiny body you barely knew would come at all, and pressed into a mucky adult clay you know will come every day, at the flick of your switch, whenever you want it. This is exactly the condition I used to avoid which I thought was impossible as poetry or anything that is the meaning I am desperate for yet now it is the only one that I make work hard; 5. Whatever manoeuvres in repression we fund in the short term will prove invaluable in the event of revolution; after the menacing from Blair Gibbs, the head of crime and justice at the Policy Exchange, who said, in response to the disclosure that police overtime payments went up by 29% between 2002 and 2006, that overtime payments have "spiralled out of control", we can suggest that the case for overtime is implicit in the need to be prepared in case the revolution should come at night; the clearance of the square is a practical demonstration of the inadvisability of imposing restrictions on overtime payments; 6. A modest spike in public fear would begin to compensate Rupert Murdoch for the embarrassment we caused him, right at the very sensitive moment when he and Jeremy Hunt were trying to consolidate his control of the British media, when it was revealed in the press that we had hushed up the phone hacking under Andy Coulson at the *News of the World*; a stimulus to petit bourgeois paranoia is best delivered at the eleventh hour, albeit at some inconvenience to the editorial staff, because the stimulus is naturally more potent the more convincingly the hooligans can be shown to have taken things too far and gone on too long, and in the case of a painstakingly slow containment operation still in progress when the news coverage ends for the night, they will have no choice but unarguably to have done just that; this is another natural basis for ringfencing overtime payments; 7. It will be an exquisite additional goad to Gaddafi and Mubarak to make them watch the police of their enemy doing with geometrical impunity what the police of Benghazi and Cairo weren't allowed to do; in some small measure it will help convince the Chinese that the pressure we exert on them in public over human rights really is just for the purposes of domestic political propaganda back home, which may yet lead to a thawing of relations between Vodafone and China Mobile; it sets a good example to the Irish, whose need for Spartan repressions in fulfilment of the terms of the loan we obliged them to accept from us could surely be made the basis for a new international market in police consultancy, right there on the ground in a bona fide tax haven; 8. Given the currently high profile of the Yvonne Fletcher murder, and in view of their being asked to dismantle a strategic analogy with what may as well be the Middle East as a whole, it may be possible for the clearance team to hallucinate that they are avenging the corps by truncheoning the Libyans; whether the team really does have that hallucination or not is arguably immaterial, since for our part it need not be true in order that we may enjoy the irony of imagining that it is, or laughing benevolently at the thought that the team might really be wrestling with spectral Libyans; the hooligans meanwhile can be allowed to achieve one part of their program, namely that they turn into spectral Libyans when you remind them of the repressibility of their *jouissance*. These meanings are not yet all equivalent, some do that better than others. If you stop and think about it, it might contribute to the pacification of the EDL, who can be expected to get a real kick out of seeing a bunch of pampered socialist Islamophiles compressed into a cameo of the herd which they obstinately refuse to acknowledge exists and runs politics, which may mean less budgetary nightmares for management colleagues in Luton. The meanings are not less articulated for ending up unnumbered. After all accumulation is about finally not remembering what meaning you are on, or not caring, but not caring turns out to be a treacherous attitude, best done on the sly, because all your care is radiant. Know your fucking enemy.

II

As sure as any air must spread the cost of any breathing
head thrilled out to cold perfection released from its
protection to keep our estimates so rough that each can
lean in close enough to bind on to the other free and
blind to her obscurity so every paralysis condemns to
cost analysis terminable or not the same live instrument
of breath and blame the high demand is prod the speck
to check its balance on the neck restructured not to
bend or turn or lose what might be saved to earn a
personal account of how in love with what it can't
allow either to be or disappear their average becomes
more dear loaded with phony fire to drown desire as
the blood slows down to last forever missing out as
mirrored in the late bailout or ever wash away the
smear of values else in sight too clear to stare in lucid
vanity transfixed to our insanity whose stalk is knotted
on a nail of sex smashed in too deep to fail or go for
just as long as wait or last a whole life wrong too late
but soft enough to trim the lips no kiss too infinitely
grips since sadly being shoved away is what makes
yesterday today disprove tomorrow shining more
robust than ever on the floor as managers are first to
know by shadowing the afterglow that blurs as
irrepressible desire or inaccessible is thrust hard at a
new mock dot whose proxy for the vacant cot assigned
its pun in Eliot is packed in silica crystals to desiccate
essentials for bare minds wintering in jars of skulls
bussed in from empty bars rebutting dusters in a fridge
not plugged in a dismantled bridge but switched on at the
wall and shut in protest at the power cut impatient
for pneumatic joy since emptying that girl or boy on
tips of absence getting hard to drink in yards of cooling

lard in envy of their hotter love of all our suffering above the Hotpoint *silex scintillans* the bright spark libertarians who lisp over the drone sublime get high on gore and moral rhyme and scheme on ideal felonies and bogart hash on balconies to level all disparities in passion only once as fuck so flashy bankers snore amok who split apart in bliss to ply the sexy shrapnel satisfy the universal appetite for more orgasmic natural right whose aspic and preservatives sustain neoconservatives to scavenge under god in blood and liberate his wavy flood Januzi UKHL 5 will keep the flagging law alive cement forever wet in dreams of Tigris' disemboguing streams of bonded revenue and dust shored up with picturesque disgust by poets mindfully concussed the more content the less unheard as vision sways its best when blurred suffice to say and get ignored like genitals too hard and bored for all the time you wait and break or mend to die will only make the memory of difficult passionate love still more occult and tender faces disappear as lost mist leaves a mirror clear to vanish yet permanently diminish not so passingly as love must in a slighted head shut up in dreams admired instead of shed like jobs to multiply the way out by the inward cry for fleecy care or finny drove or feather'd youth or all my love or scaly breed since with that shit Iraq in general must grit its icy core of heart and mind in not just spectral abstract rind but profit for the vested rim who mass produce the phantom limb rip open markets in despair mock cannibals who bite the air rinse spit and flush their sacred founts and whine about the body counts.

Still wringing the still obvious thing for side to side
hard pressed ears ring up inside sales in justice scales
by invoicing their vanished males in arabesques that
Sky regales or JP Morgan rigs to drip on Qtel for the
Gaza Strip when god in heaven trickles down relieving
Blair and turning brown the olive trees are burning
down the neck detached at no dispute the settlements
are absolute I ask a wreath fit on so hard the brain is
crushed like upstart lard deposited in spongy rats who
make our doctors bureaucrats mock children up as
innocents to prosper as their effluents and gnaw on
skulls in cellars stocked with shadows by the awed
and shocked.

Once Assyrian spivs, now votaries of natural election,
body odour clinging to the old regime, solicit for a pro
forma conscience in the sentimental porno form of an
eyeball rammed inward, to represent age; whether a
costly service when in lives or no less trenchant words,
a spent horizon dripping its limbs, parts and labour,
transacted to a cosmetic mouth embroidered with
intrinsic labia, silk teeth, outsourced love history or
cosmic dark, on the street whose massy brains lay
down to block the music drains, delivering the flood;
but what is vital and deep in me is escalated to a
surface for affixation to my sanity, reaching into a
deterrent void of mental shining after intertwisted
lights I press down on to mean your face is coming
back.

If meaning isn't obvious the brain gets mean and
envious. The revolution too bourgeois to come. An

always new but shut curtain, peeled by her single hand, behind which waits a face you wait to pull for being dead, is beautiful when shut by her double; it makes the window further away or not there at all so you definitely vanish in it. As by focus on what is apparent, art is dead labour too, all that can be done or said to end. Eat courtesy of nausea eight hours per day or longer. Go for Starbucks at Shenzhen on weekend. The very existence of a minimum wage is a very existent cage for my mum. Since I will not again be free to fall in absolutely or to delete or moderate desire for a touch whose sound is not to be believed but as dissembled to a cracking light, you are lost, stared at like distant fire through a screwed up eyelid, since that is what loss really is for Hutus and Israelis, the waxing ode indulged unto redundancy of ear; make the love that makes you disappear but at the same time instantly come back when kissing obliterated in bright agony to a grated shin or inimitable chewed-up spat-out shining spine, not desperate because alone, flooded with the only air required, shattering joy contradicts quantitative easing, replenishment of liquid life that punctually runs out, to bar us in temptation and to keep the flesh wrung dry; pure and fundamental to our blood sucked in sucked out and sucked off at RBS to fuel one man's innovative cost synergies you end up all spunked out ABN-AMRO minus LaSalle due diligence lite by lip sync, cuckolding Barclays, writing off 1.5 billion which could have gone into wells and malaria vaccines, no credit losses anywhere in the portfolio, the problem was the complexity of the products, asking what is your core equity tier one ratio on a lookthrough basis, as if to say, what the fuck are you not looking at or not through what at lumps of ice and tears is the contrite reply, shelled out from the eternal RBS reserves implicit in a trap sky of overweening negligence, while out the door the rest live past desire filing left to right, doing the cleaning and food, a plunging sky inside now too opaque to block, a sum too cryptic for the universe.

What the fuck are you on about the demilitarization of syntax? Anders Hoegstroem or whatever your concept is. An advert in amateur smoke trail calligraphy for a special edition of *The Sun* containing a photograph of a male cock ejaculating a human mouth incompatible with an organic face made to sag like what would to the averagely astutely cynical loss adjuster be hardly rotten if manifestly soaked floorboards in a style that is evidently senile but drilled in joy on every page 3, whose page count approximates infinity, all of them called 3, except for a solitary page, very close to the end, a mystery, a page called something else, a bonus page, an inextinguishable laminated palimpsest of the lot of them on which in an infant hand are artlessly scrawled in triangles the stupid words simplicity fuck and fire. What escape fuck are you on TL the demilitarization of syntax? Anders whatever 6 discharge your concept. A predictably instead of problematically predictably lovable adventure cage with no manifest theme for a domestic rat with a wire wheel pinned in it for it to run around in and translucent coloured plastic tubes pushed in it for it to slide down in a straight line or in a spiral and an opaque plastic ball in it that its child locks shut for it to run around in like a baby planet in a universe with no rat in it, representing the conscience of Lord Goldsmith. What fuck you, the demilitarization syntax bun escape? L1. Anders escape cape landscape, whatever concept. P. The colophon first significantly, then insignificantly, then neither significantly nor

27

insignificantly omitted on the in any case long ago torn out opening page of Aeschylus's *Paedos in Speedos*. Fuck you, demilitarization. TL61P. * Tearing up the rule book just aestheticizes it into a vorticist collage of General Franks. You knew that from the instant you escaped; beautiful highbrow heel-dragging in unwaded war blood will not drown it. Go and fucking smash the world to bits. A branding exercise, thrashed out over a briefing document, excluded from the minutes. 6. The concept of a life is art, as well in the White House as if not. Sincere, tho' prudent; constant, yet resigned; but *not* in jail. General Franks will not to jail, however you collage him. Unoriginality is as old as the hill, and yet as insipidly venerable. Vomit the antidote, put the salad back barely touched, mute the flares, sand off the moisturizer, extricating what it may unconvincingly be pretended are incomprehensibly stubborn last globules still there after hardly the toughest rubbing fails with the glowing tips of safety pins, pick up every shred of rule book and diligently glue it back together, edge to edge.

III

Dance down the hill. We know for a fact that the tabloids are a protection racket for politicians, so we know that voting *is* extortion. Limp up the hill. But since the alternative, in any case not yet even on offer, is fully inflated politicians too big for rackets, bigger with wind than the distended dead end of an abdomen of the sugar-coated bloated Ethiop Aeolus, so that for the time being extortion it is. Both paralyses are best sublimated into an antisocial involuntary gag reflex at the least reference to anything but last resort, a dream in which you get to wish for things which you can't think you are told you never ought to wish for, gravely flagging up the hardly flapping haggard tongue. The natural ecumenism of the press complaints commission is on the face of it the nocturnal emission of the independent police complaints commission, nicely cold and wet; the otherwise eternal compassion of the independent for what is radiant, fresh kids smash up the porn shop scattering its bitty windows over the aisles of flatpack noumenal genitals, trashing shit love; the tax return of the independent police of the future. Outer space is deeply inanimate.

Happily eat the boiled hyenas but omit to suck dry their dark alarming skulls. Capitalism, the system for profit we all die under, is the infinite multiplication of values; the last resistance is sterility, but not the least. Queering war. Thousands of unshrinking eyes rush out a split open head in a prophetic geyser, stare back as wide and bright as the whole world, plunged in thunder over us, the ochre and lavender glow of the virginal streaking sun illogically scars their billion idiotic retinas. MAKE LESS, BE MORE.

Pope's descents to Beckett's dips, Keats astride a grave betimes, a Nigerian sex slave. A Nigerian sex slave plying its overstretched, hedged, oily ass at the dusty fringes of the *Biennale* to drunk sponsors of the European tents. Or what will not debase so much as shatter, or what will not rejoin but soon rip up, or rearrange with gratuitous violence, undo savagely primp or outright annihilate. Our amity is fitted for division. You won't say anything more radical than sex. But this irrepressible oral craving for the exciting controlled annihilation of values and invariably the long concomitant impatience at their boring slow debasement over the course of natural inflation over the course of things just going on not yet with the alacrity to be interminable makes the poet a predictable stupid rake, a programmed profligate courtier, his lyric on the fucking make, his infancy a mucked up fake, all ugly sex and textbook camaraderie and floor, and all the more derisory for sadly being poor.

The meaning of pornography when I am a child is that people really meant that, in that I would, and that I could join them, either by doing it for real later, or by doing it as a fantasy *right now* instead; coming with someone who would be real but not you in the future, or coming over you right now because you are not real. Intensity makes freedom an illusion: the present is irresistible; Reality is never worth the wait. The meaning when I am a child is the same one now. Intensity makes freedom an illusion; on one cover there was a childish sketch of a cock in my mother's hand. But under the other, my secret woman with the piercing mad hole; It is worth the wait. Because of this explicable hole in the end I speculated I'd get hard if ordered to stand hovering all night over tacks, while tethered to a pillar by the wrists in some vanished friend's mother's lounge to be inspected with explicit apathy from the sofa in the end as in reality I was, every night, in my mother's hand, and at last painfully pushed down by him into the bliss at the end of this fantasy, driving the tacks in after all that long agony to avoid it; because either you split me in two or fuck you. Do not leave me only whole.

Pigging out on leverage in Merrill Lynch is the new
Charles Olson. Flesh gets hard, sadly get used to it.
Without it you imperishably shine. Values have to be
fucking annihilated. It's not enough to do Pound in
indifferent voices wisecracking to your banker crony
about "the upjut of sperm" in a parody of an admission
of inferiority to see whose spontaneous pornography
can repudiate sex best, *quia pudendum est*. You at the
back, cremate me, quick. Resuming all your days and
splatter on the hallucinated mouth you sadly drool a
window on, yet throw it wide to let a breath sheer in;
once the breath is beautiful; The same old same old
up the you know what; Brief contact is not irritating
But prolonged contact, as with clothing wetted with
material, May cause defatting of skin or irritation, seen
as local redness with possible mild discomfort; The
oral suspension cannot hold the benzoates you only
dream: *Verfremdungseffekt* by arbitrary searches.
Lashed on thrashing fire inside like flashing flutes of
Gaviscon. I want to get rid of the squint, but how? How
to go numb from lisping in numbers? And how really,
not like that. If this is the way that this sentence
resorts to your head, why know otherwise? Where's
the oversight? Whose tribunal? By involuntary spasms
reality pushes you out, banging on the wall. There join
me Muses, in the songs of triumph, flying the friendly
skies, like this. What do you think of this bit, Bill?
Is it just a UPC for cramp, a one-liner about a crab
breathing white out? Blowing bubbles and popping
them with her claws, unconscionably erotic? Would
you first rip up then glue back together the words or the
letters? Why do you keep coming to me in dreams?
Climbing as if sideways back through the skew of
black and nothing like a midriff in your colour, not
dead for a change, not now abolished except in photos

that are also abolished, but living in the form of what
you are to me? I want a topical penis.
Excoriation of destiny is a cure for being impossible to empty,
a hoover bag in Sapphic drag, rehearsing our suction on dust.
In a closed circuit like mortality the last word is guaranteed;
it is by definition what you always get, that's the beauty of it.

     Living stops to fit the empty
cap on your desire, right
     minded to allow the sight
to fade in blinded appetite.

     Telling you again in level
voices to be stable for,
     unlistenable outside the door
to profit but to turn to shit.

     So what are you waiting for
me for, the hot shrinkwrap
     disoriented in your lap,
once believed-in, only savage?

     Fire comes on that won't go
out along the way you run, yet
     made to last for what you let
go past you, burns the eye alive.

     But look at these caricatures,
numb by numbers, empty shells,
     new complexity doorbells,
jokes about what they are.

III

Whatever the point is, it's here to stay; and there's a lesson in that for us all, if we're not too proud to pretend there is. But in a flash we are only too proud. You ask yourself if you can be excused. In the future my ghosts will multiply the more people I know die, and my ghosts will multiply more quickly the more people I know die quickly, the SKU for everyone alive is EV-A, and the rate of multiplication will grow quicker until in the end the future is nothing but my ghosts, not even me; this is a comic poem, scatterbrained Iraqis. I would run words together like wall gashes strips, thinking I'd be right. But the outcome would not be, but something else just dumped on it instead. Years of my life wasted on war, depressed and miles away. *Je le vis.* The menu bar and buttons are displayed above the text fields: The line below shows many product codes; Use the menu bar to choose commands: In addition to the standard menus; File, Edit and View, there is also the: Dialog toolbar for fast access to frequently used commands in the toolbar can be activated and deactivated at the point View Toolbar. As for humanity, right now, it can be ignored or converted into a better problem – be degraded into a problem that was bound sooner or later to give rise to solutions like government, such as the present one. The public loves to be told that it has to learn to expect less, because everyone wants everyone else to have less, and everyone is willing to have less if that is the price for ensuring that everyone else but him has less. What a cunt.

The contemporary universe is strictly undersexed.
Same principle as the banking disaster,
one love used to leverage another,
one life more renamed the next.
Elastic shoulders imitate
the shimmer of no arc itself; screaming
Don't leave your unwanted love
over the floor and run away
where what you say is what you do
without including less of you, pay attention
the fire drill in the family quad at lunchtime
is not cancelled in the end. You know that because this is
the end, and it is not cancelled yet; I will
likely not ever meet anyone I love so much as
you again; but I want to try some men before I die.

1.3

The upside of the credit crunch is the defence review.
Think of it: the damage to Britain's military standing,
the 4 billion on Nimrods (O fret not after knowledge),
the limitation of the maximum enduring army force, no
more ratification by depleted uranium of the endless
moral ringing in the ears, having none of it, no new
material for the infinite ad campaign for the new
millionth Olympian, a pedalo of foam dropped on a
laughing amputee. You go downstairs to watch *Ladies
of Letters*, pumping the wound. And why not end it
there, courtesy of paranormal disgust? Look straight
in the eye, as under it you climb through that dream grated
in returning, livid end, far into the shape I
kept in order that I could love it too late later, my eyes hurt
in my heart, too much to stare at your gently dead face its
lips removing silence from the air they brightly shun

in an impenetrable hole full of conclusive human darkness.
My head does that, I am forced and even proud,
pulling you back to precision, to life by colour,
we're allowed because you're dead and I'm older,

Shakespeare said love moderately
as mine as no-one ever was
    that line in "late Wieners"
impressing no-one, timing out.

My own heart still beats hard
at the open door to know
    who will swallow it below
the meteor imprisoned in stars.

Both routes out the window lead
to falling deaf to heavenly
    pretence but by flying only
too late into trust in deafness.

Which makes it all the more real
but hard to beat, abiding in
    despair that love will not begin
when you do, but in everything.

ODE TO TL61P 3

1.1

Loss grows more absorbent as the swelling drains
for good. Soft extinction beds down in a drone fit
to repeat. But ripped an echo, rounded up to musical
remorse. Floor as lids and wind for eyes, unsparingly
not faced. Parting like a judgment with the sky,
yet to come home. Agony lubricious as the Delta of
Niger. Life retorts a triangle, the corners flare and boil.
Inconsequence runs out and flows away like level rain.
Fuck the waxes, shaves, implants, jerking, convulsions
and sperm, real sex is the insatiable silence underneath.
Nothing but the rest is ever whole; your distance isn't real
or that unreal. Starting again is like failing to stop, the
next fat lot of untold skin-deep trillions in derivatives,
beloved surfaces bed in too deep to rip you off; The
corporate thugs are conniving to stifle the state, to
thwart its withering; the spirit thugs are conspiring to
debase all of the currencies left; outside the upset
junkie screams to tinnitate on empty air, prorumped in
odes to plenitude not mine but sadly anyone's; the
mind is what it is cracked up to be; these thoughts are
not breathable, you are not ready to be breathed; the
call sign, Carnage 27. Every time you blink you carbon
trade, so don't blink, spit the lids out. You look out of
whatever is the technical right name for the helicopter
down on the swirling monochrome dust where in an
unmistakable and completely distinct way a man is or
three men are frantically waving his or their arms in a

spectacle plainly intended as surrender; but during consultation with the military lawyer it emerges that enemy combatants cannot surrender to aircraft; you are in a tight corner; you squeeze the trigger and look watchfully at scraps of ripped-up human fucked at random into the dust. 80% and rising of hellfire missiles in Iraq were fired *after* the surge. Later, but there is no later, it will be obviously for the best, or have been, as a single dot is if weirdly craved as nothing in the universe but a single dot. Is this my work? This guess I will never be done with? Not the wage labour I do my best to ram my bed, dissolve my flesh, scratch my head, suck to climax and winnow my fingernails, contract my genitals and stay broadly sane in for money every day, or in truth not every day? The light of that day will slide in at the back of the window at first on a glassy outside but then in across intimate backs and through fronts and will evenly spread through the air, transparently retinal burn, the glimpse of renewal to token retarded despair, with the sun in your eyes.

ground to splitting air, the poor should live where they can afford to not where they are, redistributive justice; it became a country *full* of torture, omnivorous ravenous gut for riveting blood, rigid Muslim centrefolds, radical grievance pornography, there are some porn films in which a woman is only fucked in the ass, for anyone who cares. What she is insinuating you employ her to project is hard to specify; if anyone is listening, you do your best to get to the truth of it, but if nobody is listening then it seems less important to go for a truth that needs to be got to; after all you are not showing off; you can use the old one, what you really want is not to be the genitals fucking her ass, but to be her, to own the ass and be entitled to withdraw it; or it, open but entitled to be withdrawn; to be passive and open and plastic and traded in light; and because in the end virtual exploitation is for consenting adults less toxic than real, on condition that on principle you do not pay for it; and since in the end with every increment of market deregulation, nilpotent or not, the superannuated neoplatonism of that old distinction grows more and more scratchy and kitsch, until, which is to say, so that, its value comes back round again; so, the meaning to desire is that sexual excitement about the exploitation of women in pain is less deplorable the more unironically it can be extenuated by the collection of its conceptual debt to the always already widespread commodification of vicariousness and its outstretched rims of transgression, Enron to Xbox, either in this case and in general, the more widespread the more inviting, on top of whatever it also owes to the will to abjure the organ responsible for pain, as also in its turn for love, in this case and in general.

1.2

Reactionaries think life should mean life. You don't believe in rehabilitation. Everyone is alone when she orgasms, caressed into an empty word. On screen during my existence, and in the last analysis in lieu of it, a really beautiful woman is explaining that Britain must be prepared to fight to retain Thatcher's European budget rebate. *Selah.* Giddy detestation of senior liquidity managers, strong aversion to strategy consultants, deep disgust at lead auditors, growing impatience with industry relations directors, spasmodic shrinking from financial modellers, rational fear of property loss adjusters, slight suspicion of corporate accountants, psychedelic distrust of branch compliance officers, agitated antipathy for growth managers, ancient nausea at contract administrators, dinky distaste for equities client service heads, labile abomination of senior enterprise application architects, melodramatic dread of heads of international payments, cute dismay over dispute consulting vice presidents, cocky chagrin at directors of pricing strategy, wholesome horror of reporting and valuations accountants, inevitable irritation with fund controllers, mawkish mortification by renewables project finance associates, happy hostility to high yield analysts, untakeable misgivings over multi-billion dollar special situation fund junior analysts, smart dislike of debt finance associates, rambunctious loathing of fertilizer traders, shitty animosity for corporate finance generalists, implacable deprecation of fund placement relationship managers, depressed estimation of equity derivative confirmation drafters, blind rage at trainee futures traders, greasy disapproval of sell side analysts, imperative repugnance at flow rates desk strategists, sclerotic conflict over front office generalists, unschooled coolness on arbitrage traders, fussy disfavour of clearing margin managers, bent enmity with solutions specialists, elegant spurning of heads of securities, fevered shuddering at exotic rates associates, being discombobulated by top tier attorneys, attitudinistic trashing of prime brokerage associates, involuntary flinching from algorithmic traders, iffy qualms with quant developers, instant revulsion at options data analysts, hard-won hang-ups about life and health actuaries, automatic melancholy when confronted with corporate actions specialists, nuclear abhorrence of continuity managers, petty incredulity at transitions co-ordinators, complex disaffection for performance improvement operations professionals, real hatred of transformation managers, waning displeasure at heads of decision support, discreet pique at heads of client integration, evangelical vexation at asset servicing specialists, irresponsible annoyance about transfer agency operations managers, fruitless fretfulness over distressed debt fund analysts, mealymouthed misdoubt of credit sanctioners, overdue animus for debt markets writers, harrowed disbelief at credit partners, plangent repudiation of restructuring reporters, gruelling denial of structured credit surveillance analysts, necrotic mockery of assurance managers and irremediable illness of disposition toward regulatory affairs consultants getting social housing down to the last unfuckable man means that you don't really want the communism you say you want. For only something has to change and fast. You can't love everyone because you can't do all the billions of different types of love. Do the wrong one and you'll never forget it.

Since not a single song I made is comprehensible to you, I think I must be too bourgeois or indigent to praise you. One song that was never sung you archived for me in the breast, unlistenable outside it, meant strictly for consolation, when as the inconvenienced heart is turned off and the world erased it scruples on its part in peace not squandered but in heaven.

   it is a good ear and it has been licked allegedly hard but it will not fly in payment for the annealed ultimate fragment of empty fridge or vagrant spigot to ultimately glut on later sublimed into a loss leader whose collateral loss is implicitly infinite, in instalments, for in your defence it turns out the whole kitchen was always and on purpose roughly this unsalable,

whatever sort of incredibly weird noise it mutes in peace
signs
/
lost to how I matter, ignorant of the youth of paradise
the hummingbird cell, machine guns everywhere
you look. AQI actually using mentally handicapped
persons to attack coalition forces. They used exploding
women from the attic. Poetry evolves from a vivid
play of nerves and confusions into sedative aporiae in
mock-heroic marginalese, if you don't take precautions
to prevent it. Maturity is learning not to flinch at childish
swipes and kicks, to know when harm is seriously
meant. The really beautiful woman who is yet to explain
how I should fight to retain Thatcher's rebate is now
bent over into a suggestion about how to prop up the
euro; I can see into her womb.

*

It's dark in there, Deborah. Whatever I am doing
now, it gets a part in there; I cannot see why else I am
not here. The void is to my left and not in front of
you at last. In the future, which is the front for too
late, there will be a virtualalium where you call up
everything left in the entrance; everything I am was lit by
love, but is now independently bright, on account of being
perceptible as it is; social justice prevents adequate
concentrations of capital. When you get older, genitals
grow less interesting; spited, the integral glass
forever fades into its shattering finish, dictating erotic percussion,
as love no less appears to end
but nothing can retard that turn
as fear that it will disappear
like antiseptic on a burn
to speak for the rampant Polish doing our dead end jobs in bed

by dreaming of us; but the reason it's that
way is what will keep it that way, to own pleasure unthinking,
to live another day and kill the rest, a skimmed-off sky on fire
unpractised in desire to stay put.

Death please spare me over for another year, your life
depends on the favors of man. But he turned out
to be a sex slave. That was how class boomed before
everyone subverted the theoretical structure of it.
Imagine whatever you think is affordable housing,
now imagine why anyone should get it. I'm never scared
to be alone any more, but I will never give up; just as
a tragedy is something you are obliged to imagine must
be capable of teaching you something, and a comedy
is something you are not obliged to imagine must be
capable of teaching you anything, so you are not
obliged to imagine you keep just knowing this, taking
it, making it up, or doing nothing, least of all for a living;
all the times you came from what I did in a row make an
alternative eternal life feel possible not as stand-up but
in fact; just as, so that those now abandoned moments
of joy can have a supplement in the form of cavities
that you can't stop playing with, holes for your most
private microvilli, the damages are temporary because
they seem so forever, by convincing you that they
always do. What it feels like is a game, one where you get
life after life; but though you go back to the beginning
whenever you want and make it more auspicious by
knowing what you have to do on the later levels, you
never get to what the German philosopher G. Dubya
Hegel in a pleasingly more hyperprolactinemic
connection once called *das Unwankende*, a word also
used in Nietzsche in connection with Apollo on the
pretext of his inflexible detumescence.

The same shortfall would later be the spoilt brain child of the wife of King Yorgo of Greece, in her hypnopompic pseudohallucination on the surgical countertransference of her own clitoris and its ego; one of the Napoleons will do a sponsored spin in his shallow grave of scrambled dolphin egg, one-way mirrors, for every explicit dousing in caustic of the Romantic subject on flexitime you do in an uproariously automated language game incontinent of its only concept and contemporaneously versified with stylishly conscious if not on that account deliberate ineptitude in order to be eulogised at symbolic profit as the *last* last farce of the authentic middle class subject in America, to boost property values in its most desirable urban centres, the flagging flagship flarf salons of New York universalism.

if that is what it takes, to live by blunting futility;

we look at each other's parts under the table, Jackie and I, hiding our eyes in the heads we come with, so as by the beautiful misidentification of excitement with fear to remain children forever, a proof of endurance that entitles us to be only now for the first time disconnected from one another, anywhere on earth; I don't know who she is or what she amounted to, I haven't seen her since then; she may be tied up in a Fallujah basement in nothing but a hood, toe-separators and a face dildo; but whatever she is thrilled by now, and whatever she lives in fear of, I trust in truth that somewhere beneath all the real objects there still shines to her distraction the first image of the male genitals I gave her, wrongly flickering, spitting blanks, preserved in trailing clouds, tiny and perfect, the origin and corner of my love. I am also charmed with many points of the Turkish law, to our shame be it spoken, better designed and executed than ours; particularly, the punishment of convicted liars: they are burnt in the forehead with a hot iron, being proved the authors of any notorious falsehood. I should go on to tell you many other parts of justice, but I must send for my midwife. If you read Marx when you're stoned, it sounds like Beckett: "Grace to be born and live as variously as possible."

*

All three parties whipped their members. Invisibility spreads up from the hand into the arm and shoulder, so that the economy resembles an archaic torso whose python is thus at liberty to ingurgitate its lyre; love is very childish to the point of no return; there is, merely there must be, in the universe a planet identical to the one you are on, but for the solitary adjustment that the person who is you on it now and who was already you on it when you were still here on this, and who will be you here on this when at last you are there on it, if you are, has never once agreed to indecipherably blur, not for a second there, or less, into anything that is worth being merely about you, nor ever once asked if you are here, now, on this, are you there, or what you are here on this for if you are, or why you are not yet on that like he is, and doesn't drink like you do here, or smoke so much drugs, and for such a good reason that the mere rumour of its existence is a light whose dimmer is natural broken, that neither of you get. Rummage while adrift, fixate when you get back. That's the epic of thought, recollected by memory like an apron string; TL61P sentimentally hacked into the bark with a sterilised syringe full of futures and eggshells. How do you reconcile wanting to be as big as possible (within credible anatomical limits) with the indisputable reality that you were very small in the beginning, where love was primary and not pegged to the dollar or spoiled by being a replacement, except by adamantly filling up a beloved person until it hurts rather than barely impinging on her in embarrassment like a spongy earplug rested on a cross-section of mushy pea? I put Christian in my mouth under the blanket, played with him as if gargling. I didn't know what to do, so it felt better, authentically childish. I had to sleep in his bed because my mother put me there, as if killing our father; I could hear her sobbing downstairs at being stood up but not listen to it. Later that night I had to have been asleep. He asked later that we keep it secret, once we had learned that you can do that. I was fine with that, though I also felt that it was somehow melancholy that such a simple act of pleasure between people still roughly equal at that age should need to be made into a source of fear, when all we had to fear was other people, who could surely be imagined to come under the same blanket; I wanted everybody to get something out of my mouth. What comes from it now is this ode, bright abolition to apathogenesis; I stare at the white screen wanting to know what comes of it next, or later; and whether I am living or dead depends on you, and when you read it; it depends who you are, like tides on the moon, blood on the measured heart.

1.3

Dying will not mean wasting your life but bearing to pass for nothing. It means not waiting for life to bear in the past for nothing else. Whatever is nothing but next to come, bearing is intrinsic. You learn it inside out then disappear, or are probably outside already. But how is outside when the difference sets to bear the nothing there. The point is not to unlearn love, try to love nothing. It stops too strictly infinite: attrition must be sung fuck that: each and every loss of it will mean the edge away: mean your life but nothing else, love for nothing gets it true. Passion must be learned back start to end infinitely or your life will end without you.

> The ratings cut to junk PDD-NOS ratings
> triiodothyronine parts shortages, it shall
> be you lashed naked short; a tight borrow
> fire engineering Lehman pre-junk libidinous
> prongs, solid waste TDO PID 6 ratings go
> gloat fit to fringe;

and once more to live and grow
    as one by what we never give
enough of any life for, but
    rejoin us by refusing love

to memory will fake and spin
    apart synthetic as smashed in
more readily is hard to prove,
    the answer is not right needed.

As on the missed and single way
    refusal is its own reward,
my best of you who are of me,
    and minded its eternity.

Drag her off the sofa and up the stairs. I do want to hear that, I do want its reimbursement, I don't want to ignore how it also says what I don't; but you begin to know that the iron *would rather* be left on, acting on a blind impulse to claw back *anything* to fetishize; until finally, the flow of that progress is now and then more or less imperceptibly interrupted by a bucket of sand, bunking off a work-song on the bourgeois bogus fringe. Your mother's tongue a prod of junk, her chin in a flying cowpat. What do you mean as if you are beautiful? I mean as if you never disappear. Will it equally prove nothing? I can still imagine what it would be like to see your face moving about and breathing, breaking open with laughter, a harmless shadow on your neck, taking your drugs with me, then mine, floating in the bathroom; you grow up as a flower in my head; you had a moderately big ass; you wrote pretty surrealist pornography about your love to me; I could at least pretend to be able to say anything to you, and believe in what I knew was the pretence while it lasted by not credibly acknowledging it, and you could do the same for me; but now you're gone, and I'm the government. But really you're just away. The music of the ice cream van is scrunching up the hill of tar, don't be ordinarily afraid; liberals want the state to be a way of life. But we suffered as a society from being too optimistic, we thought the good times would last forever. That led to the de facto socialization of credit, rather than what I wanted at the time, and still want now, and may yet definitely want forever, the planned socialization of labour, so that the payout of immiseration wound up infinitely deferred. That mistaken epic of bad socialization is the material base for the late deconstructive superstructure, a mind impressing limits nicely warped but going flat. The rest of us, if you can believe that, are best abandoned to trade our way through clinical depression in infamous cycles on that fat roundabout with the mat. Think of the things you bring home and cram into your house, and all still there. What rips apart the ironed sheet to find its messy face asleep, dreaming of the Congolese reserves. But the private sector will take up the slack, by genustupration of the levers of fiscal power that operate the rack, taking up the blessed strain of ownership from Iraq: unemployment will come stretching down. Mahler is beautiful for being as if infinitely resourceful in a climax; you want him for a meaning of his life. Bush gave evil a bad name. It's like you're still living in 1990, thinking you can have everything you want.

ODE TO TL61P 4

1.1

They brought *rapists* in to break the strike. Labour are
looking for symbolic targets to cause symbolic political
discomfort to the banks. As you get older, you learn how
to find older people attractive; sexuality is adaptive but
love is intransigent.

*

Obama wants to cleanse the US senate of filibustering.
Elsewhere the secretly mendicant unknown of Nigeriana
Director & Senior Executive Officer Peter T. S. Wong alerts
millions of perfect strangers, "we have decided that I
will have you claim this." This information is repeated
until the meaning of elsewhere comprehends it and
won't let go.

*

Fit your life on what you want, not as you abjure.
Nothing is so *had* as us, the roller floor of ruled-out
flesh, spun but to the cheapest blur; dusting out the
only once, never again sharpest corners of mental lust
again, snapping at the nail that feeds it, staring into bed
time. Attend to how that bad tone evens out.

*

What can't go on forever, show me how: the answer is

rolled out in other lines; the fish made for the fairground can't allow: the reason for its point is like a cone; asking what in the flicker under that: which you may wince to call your curvature; can be lifted,
is laid flat: the sexual soul perverted for its cure.

*

There was as fine a row of boys and girls as you ever saw; some beautiful faces, and one exquisite mouth. I said I would kiss Louise, a beauty I knew frightened me, because, if I can't escape taking it too deeply by kissing her, in the, I now say, approximate portico in concrete I knew opposite a wire fence threaded at random but distractedly with abstractions of childish plants and weed, after school; because I felt we had made a contract that must be broken to seem premature; that neither of us would go through with it; I am in that room waiting as if desperately for the lesson to end; it does and we both run to what we knew; I ran away. I never got to love Louise. I did not kiss Louise. Later I would love to have sucked her vagina.

*

Mother, when you were fucked you sang badly. Now you sing fine, never to be heard.

*

It can't be done unless you fail it too. I wanted the clouds to make it *impossible* to get down, not to be able to see *anything* on the floor, to be stuck up there with you in that freak weather forever; and do I not want the same thing now, only with a different person and no alternative precipice? There is no irony in that, it's a truth about excitement; money in the dark blue vault, the sanity of stars.

*

I'm going to *kill* the neighbours. That thumping in the walls. They'd better be having a *fucking good* time.

*

The beautiful thing about you is more than anything everything in the world I still love to do. There is a competitive advantage in remaining to be done; when I first thought them, none of these meanings was paralysed. They run and run. You are infinitely disadvantaged by persisting to the past. A dream / I dreamed you long ago, now again begun.

*

TL61P is a piece of shit – an infinitesimal piece. You barely notice it come out. You wouldn't know you're doing it, but lost behind your back. You could fit trillions of them into a rat shit, these asset values for which no vesicle is too commodious. Fuck me vapid. Professional advice to aspiring writers is often to write only the catchy first few sentences or the paragraph that really drags you in, and send that in, because your best bet is agents will give you a contract on the strength of your having attention grabbed. Your song is in the gaping booth, the ballot slip your lyre, whose missing strings attached in truth are tuned as you alone require. Over time the investment of writing in politics dries up, so that fascination in the spin cycle can be made redundant; look at Yeats. Versification burned out one layoff after another. Solemnly inhume the car keys, Apollo is randomly fucked; TL61P is a shower of lube in powdered milk: but it is an infinity too.

*

Powdered shit. Blow out the candles. Socialise the risk.

*

You can pick up social history by watching the more ambitious documentaries about the tours of Black Sabbath (careful with this).

*

I am in you like I am in my skin. Except that you burn in me.

*

The anti-war movement was too eclectic, as celebrated by the transparently liberal media; the pensioners and teenagers let down the Muslims and the SWP. There was not a basis in natural sympathy, but recreation around a core of disgust; you find the same problem for art, whose ongoing reception fades into an endless praeludium to the absolute banalisation of sacrilege. I stood on the plinth of the statue and looked at the crowd, and out over the park, at the enormous stream of people that I would make into my people, genuinely from the best motive, I was ill, and I thought that it was so large that with some intelligent coordination it could take over the city of London by passion, seizing the telephone exchange and the garrison and the armory, like Trotsky, whose portrait is now in my bedroom on top of the 1715 edition of the *Fairy Queen*, whose subscribers included the Surveyor General of the Ordnance; that's how fiction operates, magical patina all the way down; it was a threat to the state, but the state was too big; it might have worked in the Congo.

*

I keep meaning to live to the end, but you have to go on without it. After the days of rage we felt isolated and marginal, in concert with the third world uprisings. Bling your war home. The underground is all inside your head.

*

I do not blush like Pliny at our miserable origin. Face is a verb for retard; silence the verb for acquit. The fuzz box clams up stage by stage, Mount Rydal to Under Mogadishu: the point is to become transparent enough to calculate your way to the rim.

*

You see through love, and that deludes your sight.

*

Run at the end and drop the open mouth. The Sales Manager at ABC Tampa drooling over the 15 million in Romney ads is your too-busy-being-productive-to-be-incestuous father, who is decommissioned into poems mocking *Facebook* by *Facebook* generation poets

clinically dependent on *Facebook* for their unfolding
sexual self-identification, whose itchy-disgusted-wilful-
compulsive-minor-thrill-seeking in the deflective
surfaces of an anti-social real-time on-screen diagram
of diminishing human returns is also but as it were
only collaterally the hottest wellspring of capitalist
evolution, chivvying love into the form reserved in
psychological experience for the successful circulation
of blood values whose origin in elective data entry is
no reflection on their climax in the predicted hundred
billion dollar flotation.

*

Mitch McConnell wants to clear out the filibustering.
A love song to the death of intimation, the eye in flower
darkness rips its shadows in
to hide the flood of unimagined ends, the unspeakable,
unendurably too unstoppable, unthinkable human orgasm.
How perfect have been all those I have given.
How many have been all the ends I taught.

*

Make it now. They hate our way of life.

*

The coinage of paedophilia is attributed by the OED
to Havelock Ellis, who in his *Studies in the psychology
of sex* (whose first volume begins with a study in the
evolution of modesty) classified the sexual love of
postpubescent individuals for prepubescent individuals
as an "abnormality". We embraced a new ideologeme.
Since those first beginnings in what innumerable

psychoanalytical thinkers confined to the humanities can now conceptualise as the "pathologization" of too durable infant desire, keeping up childhood for too long, our machinery of classification has been melodiously refined. Besides paedophilia, which now means the sexual love of prepubescent individuals in particular, we now have hebephilia, a diagnosis for the sexual love of individuals in the early stages of puberty, but not earlier; ephebophilia, a diagnosis for the sexual love of individuals lately progressed out of puberty (these last two are sometimes also called korophilia and parthenophilia); teleiophilia, a diagnosis for the sexual love of adult individuals, whom we mirror; and gerontophilia or graeophilia, a diagnosis for the sexual love of elderly individuals. These diagnoses are in turn the subdivisory disorders of chronophilia, a more general term for any limitation of sexual love to individuals living within fixed age limits; chronophilia is in turn a paraphilia, a yet more general term familiarly of biomedical application that describes the misdirection of sexual love as a whole, be it into babies, or non-human objects, or images of suffering, or corpses. It will be obvious that the history of diagnostic refinement in pathologization is at least nominally a case of clinical hellenism; hellenism is itself a word adapted out of its original meaning, which was "the acknowledging and adoring of a multitude of Gods", to fit the less immoderately orgiastic definition "Graecism" in thought or speech. The criminal use of desire would be very grating in Kurdish.

But all sex is barbaric. We *are* the pleasures we enjoy, the blisses we admire; and all sex is a text, wingbats in a gaping slang. I adopt Hazlitt's position on the immortality ode because my mother was an alcoholic.

Freud said that my early biological hermaphrodism led to my original predisposition to bisexuality, which in the course of my development was reduced to monosexuality, leaving slight remnants of the stunted sex. The idea of development truly is formidably legitimate; and yet it is only the first of many ideas, each one more legitimate than the next. My infancy was an original predisposition to sexual love for children, which over the course of our development was reduced to sexual love for teenagers, and then, as if conclusively, to the same for adults; the elderly are terminally attractive but I would rather not suck them. Infant love is as durable as life. If it isn't, it must be. Immortality must mean the preterition of ageing, so that universal love may be comprehensive, that is, paedohebeëpheboteleiophiliac (omitting the elderly, who are ostentatiously not immortal); the sum of all disorders is the law of paradise. You can disagree with it but you can't disobey it. That's the bottom line.

1.2

There is a disconnect between the people and real politics. Meanwhile imaginary life, its dead end leavened unto the breach in its primitive control order, will insist on scavenging up the one aisle of definitively unshiftable goods, absolute for a bargain; the symptom of its being a currency is not to say the point of it. These odes are an only deficiently reorderable anagram whose letters don't all move laughed at during oral sex, a subtitle for everything we are. Trotsky said that the genetic links between the cow and the ameoba are immaterial for practical thinking, since the farmer is interested only in the *individual* qualities of the udder. Ringfence the spheres, universal benefits. Never middle yet too squeezed. The problem with perfectionism in poetry is the same as it is in sex: *all* ejaculation is premature. But perfectionism once abandoned will return to make you very stupid, as if you laugh in the wind summoned as a reprimand by your mother your face will not in truth stay like that. Roman watched me glide past in a dress. I returned to the bedroom and probably did something like another line. We thought that was completely hilarious, she did and I. She kissed me in the toilets for fifteen minutes and I did the same. I laughed at that. No-one in the queue will complain because everyone in the queue enjoys being impatient to do something illegal; the wait is nonetheless too long for being intrinsic. Our pretext is that when the doorman comes we will seem to be kissing, which meant really kiss; you said my mouth was softer than you expected after passion made you think I was constructed to be rough. The problem with conceptualism duplicates the one made earlier, pornography *replaces* sex and art; its originality is its provocation. Baudelaire and Gautier were nuns compared to us, transgeneric Cambridge hashishistas. You become radical when the only thing you can do to rouse the sleeping public is something truly catastrophic. Catastrophe is the thinking man's prosthesis. His belief is that in the face of grand projects to change the world, ordinary life is dispensable; on that basis the poet is his natural ally.

*

There is somewhere in infinite space a world that does not roll within the precincts of mercy, and as it is reasonable to suppose that there is music in heaven, in those dismal regions perhaps the reverse of it is found, made sweetly by the negroes unmasked by the author of 'An Arundel Tomb', for their private functions; those who neglect to please us are not doing it properly. But of which administration could less of what be said and never heard again for what? *Obama's?* The administration of modernism is to be difficult on purpose, to love the confusion of others as much as your own. Melody is exchanged for atonality, proving their trail by fungibility; however much these words dispirit me I love the experience of making them. These feet are made for dragging. There are propositions we do in all candour believe in but would never applaud, such as that the children of Tony Blair should be trepanned, or just grow up to be miserable schizophrenics, for suspicion that silence would be left empty, or our wrists slapped off, or of sounding like a fascist. But fear is neglected, time and time again, until nothing really scares you just as previously a leaf stung all over by puslike dots mimetic of a fucking lost scream did invariably on the walk up through the house rise like a bubble high in carbonated honey on the market to get some sex, your mother in the bath next door, slumped, that ass poem by Christian Prigent; I suddenly feel dizzy, it's like my throat is mostly hanging out; phenomenology is a subterfuge for manifesting that the commodity is not primordial; Try doing it on coke.

*

Proudly insinuating that he is his own virus, "J.C." decided for the *Times Literary Supplement* that if you come across an avant-garde woman who is prepared to meet you even halfway, "you catch yourself thinking you've got it." His true Penelope comes to pick him up from Ogygia. The food energy in the typical ejaculation is 2.9 kJ, 0.0035% of the average helping of moussaka. Do you speak barbaric, or just fucking howl it? I remember wanting to go to bed with myself, my bed in particular, so that I could do anything I wanted to do, all to myself, since I knew everything I would want doing to me and who would do what. I alone would come in both my mouths. I would get down on all four knees and stretch wide my asses to invite in my cocks. One cock, *mine*, would be *way too big* for me and *way too hard*; the other, also mine, is antithetic to magnitude. Harder than a thousand bass teeth. I would talk down to myself, spit in my mouth, force me, I would grip my tongue in my ass. But I would not run my fingers through my hair or look directly into my eyes and say I love you.

*

Even Burke believed that we have no right to make a market of our duties.

*

The system is broken. We need to fix the system.
We need to fix the system. The system is broken.

*

Aristotle joked that love of people who are elsewhere is liable to be "watery". We use it for washing up the Africans, who are unfortunately not able to be omnipresent.

Vietnamization to versification, the euphuistic body count
corona of mental arithmetic impossible to crack
the bath water intransigently black,
and back. What you find there is that everything has
been left as it was. The TV on, the oil on the fridge, the
records all over the floor; but under the window a
bridge is waiting, on the face of Deborah. Moronic acid
is a triterpenoid; traumatic acid heals by division. "This
grand magician whose art commands nature has
selected for his palace nothing but this obscure grotto."
One of your last texts said that you wanted to kiss my
soul. I fall in an infinite sheet of immaculate light.

1.3

It's the 1960s. You ask to see the manager, only to be
told, gradually, patiently, in innumerable stages, that
you are the manager, and then asked, all at once, would
you like the person who is complaining to be ejected,
since it is you? We who bite the other hand are
whatever is being itself.

It's impossible to bypass the first intoxications of
sadism forever, gambling on a new age old age; you
can ask the manager if you can find her why the exit is
so dismally far away.

Olson may be followed to the universe, but not to
Yucatan; what remains of us is systemicide, the frugal
blossoming of the void.

The void is final. Children are naturally quick to fidget,
making up for their denaturation by deficiency in peace
and incest: soppy inverted Schlemihls reinventing the
wheelspin on ice.

Or on sand, belabouring Iraq, withering like the Greek
marble industry,

Daughters of catastrophe, abandoned to the moon,
I'm only reality but digging in your forehead
where reason is not the irony for you but the opposite is
true, Leonie crawling from the tent with a new virginity
that moment inherited, to declare to my owner who laughs
in sympathy and knowledge at the innocence I bring
like a baby animal into the language of adults, that I opened
myself to show her what I was down there, because she asked
for that, and I couldn't yet care what it meant
to myself that I barely had yet, or even what it meant to her,
or whether I was truly thrilled right then and there,
only that by getting out the thing she asked to see
its secrecy became its truth, and what it did for me
became its end, mirroring the primary exchange
on credit of this impossible flame, hunger not eternity;
I dissipate superficiality forever until I explode there.

ODE TO TL61P 5

1.1

I stupidly broke the catch. I slammed the door shut and
the catch encased in the door is now broken. The catch
inside the rim is fine, and if I lodge a spoon in there it
continues to function, but obviously then the door isn't
closed. I am having a nightmare finding a replacement
door. I have managed to take the door off. But I can't
seem to get the door apart to remove the catch itself. A
liquid sieve was slicked on mock extinct. The grating is
a waste grown empty, ground up in the missing cogs;
the ultimate multifacets grow facetiously immortal. For
who knows well it isn't; she wants more than that, and
so should you; please as if gradually read all the notes
on your coding notice; it's good to know the worst, it's
good to know that it's only that; Perturbation theory
leads to an expression for the desired solution in terms
of a formal power series in some small parameter that
quantifies the deviation from the exactly solvable
problem. Love can be trusted not to fade, as also faded
out to trust; devour the wind that just washes over
you, its meaning is its filling; your reflection in glass
blown into the shape of your face to accommodate its
progressive jutting; cracks appear in your shambolic
argumentative scream learnt fresh from first orgasming,
a rondo to oblivion *d'exécution transcendante*; excess
levity leads to an unblessed strain injury for the dozen
or so marketing executives secretly pretending to
get good enough at free improvisation; they're out

back; whatever the fuck that thought is, *get it back*; commissioning variations on your theme – the screen blinks, Yemen for cubist; get it back; mortality is scrambled to the précis of our meaning, to make life comprehensively succinct; the immutable is better than the mutable, the inviolable is better than the violable, and the incorruptible is better than the corruptible: look at teeth, or Africa. Or Wales. Look at yourself. You don't need to be Dante.

I go on to the mound. It is snowing a bit. The fence at the corner is obscurely associated with being loved and doing the creosoting for a meagre sum which I think is a lot but is also a way of rounding into the street with your feeling of disappointment. Twigs scratch and knock on it, later redone in local colour. People are dragging back the sled. On the top the snow is packed onto the muddy grass oddly hard by all their feet. That is the efficiency of feet. People go down the mound. In the summer when the snow was gone under the mud I went there with David and ended up agreeing to be the one who was fucked so long as I did not have to be the one who would fuck back, and put myself on my hands and knees with my pants down, in front of him, facing away; I felt myself become a hole, I now think I emerged as a hole for him; I now emerge as a hole for you. We didn't get to do it, our mothers came looking for us and stopped it even before fear did, but I suspected even then that he was frightened or just indifferently disgusted, since otherwise surely he would have done it to me quicker, since I think so; I mean that him fucking me would have come first, but not me fucking him, or our mothers; we should have made our mothers come too late; I heard that he told people about it and I was angry because I was ashamed at having again capitulated to secrecy; secrecy was my enemy, like God engrossed in someone else; in the caravan in his garden I tried pressing him to agree to one last fuck without touching with his father figure who was a man I now give a cartoon nose, white skin, a beard, and idly establish was 40. I'm colouring in his hair, it's brown. It wasn't love, but it hurt and left me complex; I am a real hole for you, not a barely noticeable flimsy crack; David had a stupid way of laughing and a fucking ugly blush. Hasten defections. I swapped stickers with him, and went on to exchange my motorbike for Christian's tank, an agreement which my father unhappily replied was a sort of extortion from infancy, but which made me sexually delight in having given away more than I had got back, for the delight was secret; I made my sister wear the fantasy lieutenant's shirt with the felt tip arrows pinned to the collar. To propitiate invasion. Nylon for Insignia. I lay under a cushion and asked her to jump on my head. She did. I like Roxette, *Elite* and cocoa butter on carrots.

10/11/10

The police smack the people in Merrion Row, doing their jobs justice; at Millbank the windows are booted down, voiding reinforcement; the government boys look set to make our solvency heroic; their genitals in plaster deck the halls like powerdrills;

You walk from the Strand to Nelson, left at the corner into Whitehall; the police are instructed to ingratiate camerapersons, by ignoring them; the technique is borrowed right from the top, tolerance of poverty is its paradigm; you film them and they film you, synergy by right;

Because the universe has been outmanoeuvred, individuals flourish; to put away your childish things, cut the arts first; say in the prophylactic tone of establishment sarcasm; what chance for debt reduction against the sheer nobility of sentiment;

If there will be a revolution in the UK, it will require the army; war will continue either way, sugared by truth or not; love is not the unswerving professional bias of police dogs; it has to be made from scratch at the first indication of its possibility.

The French have their *avantages à qui*, as we in turn have ours; a peine rentrés les lampions, voilà que tombent les bonnes; if we don't fight now, the super-rich will harden into sultans; deeply and truly fuck them, one-way receptacles;

At the corner of Parliament Square the teenagers are standing on bus shelters; they are shouting for what they believe and feeling what you never will; think of the anger you waste on gifts that might be used on money; masturbation is not love, it's betrayal of the workers;

You can see the predisposition to moderate success in politics; in the features of Aaron Porter, the flexible physiognomy; the thought of sex with him doesn't occur to the majority of his delegates; that's what makes him perfect for redefining compromise;

The wall of glass smashed in, looks like what Wordsworth saw; in the flint windbreaker, lying on the empty floor; to be a shard of broken glass, shining like life; psychosis as the mirror of your dreams, or justice;

A cop with a freshly bandaged face is the punctum of the coverage; her wide eyes make fear emblematic, glint on film intensely; at Sussex they grabbed them and chucked them down the slope to be arrested; at the bottom of the slope the women on minimum wage count the minutes of grind;

I'm far from knowing what to do about any of

this, or after it; but so long as my blood is attached to the world I live for by its motion; I create this pledge in utter solemnity, I will never deny it; but burst to make its love for everyone shower from my heart.

The west Irish had nothing but tiny scraps of land with a cabin, a pig and potatoes; but Belfast and Dublin had England. Love gets saner, stained into the glass. All countries must work together toward a mutual resolution of currency imbalances, or risk war, says the governor of the Bank of England, tasked with making the genital stage of Godzilla inevitable; but he is right, it's the answer Jesus would give if pressed; the severance will yet amount to minus sweet fuck all. Your job is to be at that orgy and to experience maximum anxiety, write, and see what happens; it's not a joke to say that you learn from that, except you decline. Synergized to social fact, surplus grout of the myriad equivalents; at the source I is screaming or am; the consummated Islamabad dispatches rolled into a prolegomenon to an epigram. Smoke that shit. *Yes.* Passion swings both ways, unfixed to be enlarged, hungry for the majority of the earth. Robert's penis is a surprise. In my tent, it is more pink than I am. I am more red or purple or brown. I had guessed, startling me, but I sucked it anyway, not to go back; I think it was an excruciation to him and a probably morally significant embarrassment, because he never used it against me when I started punching his face in on the couch at my mother pissed herself on; get it back; why did I do that, smacking around with childish fists, deepening our wishes, blunting life in him and me; or smack that miniscule nameless boy who merely explained to me that my fantasy car for sale to him could be given wheels, when I wanted it to be flat and just glide? The Victorian English had their more innocent Green Zones in India, from which to perorate on the superiority of peace for trade; indiscreet to go slaughtering around all over the place like the Russians via the French and in any case very likely more overheads to redemption. If sex is the price for that, be it what you may; after all sex disappears anyway.

Remembering nothing at all the right moments is difficult; so much of the rest of your time is exchanged for the lot; since poverty porn is the price of its spiritual opposite; what you get up to you pay for, come later; strikes are impossible unless you are quorate, don't be a speck and froth through the roof; Proudhon concealed that inflation is theft by being too famous about property; you are keeping it real; according to the definition of truth 'adequatio rei et intellectus', harmony depends on you being no better than a load of fucking things; there is no end to it; only at the end is the absolute ever what it is in truth; get what back; meanwhile regular people get impatient, adopt silence as compensation for their virtue in waiting for it; which I cannot do, and so am angry to think about; though I am not obliged to think about it; and I am not obliged to be angry either. 2. Compassion should be balanced and sustainable, like growth, not more balanced and more sustainable. Public sector workers will not solve your problem because they are net tax consumers, what you need is for people without any exposure to universalism to create the wealth. Wealth tastes better like that, anyhow. Less like Asian fusion. 3. The dream is finally to have no need of money of our own, like the government, but there is nothing to finalise; if you can't stymie their manipulations, you can settle for monitoring their surplus, but either way they're all the same, they leave you in the end for a *stärker Dasein*; a huge rope of blood the width of a golf bag falls out of his eye when you shoot into him, you are an heroic soldier; the kindness I have enjoyed has been more unusually beautiful from Hindoos than from Christians, and weirder; the very idea of a virgin birth is a slander against my sex; and yours too, whatever that is, whoever you are beside me; our tribute to the world is our desire, nothing else.

China is now a multilateral partner. That joke about the reference to the answer in the riddle in the reference to the answer to my life will be repeated without a pause until I laugh. Bush says *three* people were waterboarded, and hold the zeroes; our text today is *maintain physical integrity*, but a hundred times funnier, and therefore a hundred and one times funnier, billions of times funnier, and hereafter infinitely more funny because stupefying at a compound growth rate too big to fail. There is something we need to do about everything, something it is always hard to be. Career poets are part of the problem, smearing up the polish, drying out the fire; chucking shit all over the place; not being party to the solution; banking on the nodding head 'the reader' saying 'yes, that's what it's like' so as not to know what it's for, since meaning is easier that way, gaped at through the defrosted back window of the Audi, hence the spring for a neck; we all know where that shit got us: *being what we eat*. The British have become snobs. They don't *want* to be security guards always getting the night shifts at KFC illegally married to sewage technicians, subject to racist abuse which intelligent politicians learn they must not be seen on camera to regard as bigotry; the immigrants are real because they do. They say, I am more realistic than you. But at least you listen. The EU ones are the mainstream, the non-EU ones the avant-garde.

The real cause of massive growth in the size of the state was fighting major wars: the majority public sector is the wages of justice for crushing the fascists.

Kissing softly round the true
hole cut out of sanity
the eyes I crossed out in a fantasy
shine right through;
to burn out the profounder hole
resolved to being dead
to love complaining in your head
in your soul;
our meaning is not an indulgence
or capital all our blood
distorting like a seed to bud
in vengeance;
our representatives will crush
their lungs up like a piston,
the Cheese Lenin grates his fist on
your toothbrush,
which I take for a sex toy, friction
conceptually bleeds
into agony, the fire feeds
its fiction;
the faces are all safely tucked
in balls of knotted dream,
make the mystery face scream
or get fucked;
what in either case they sing
only as they go
back to block up the thing you go
mad needing.

1.2

Reconciliation with your mother on top of Spinozistic macroeconomics. What's
the intractable thing you did? Splitting to the eye,
whose camera will zoom in, you're meant to
brood, Fuck wish-fulfilment.
The light of truth to life back at wavering
blackout bypass. Possibility
is apocryphal impossibility. Neither is the best,
Take what's coming to you. Massification
is light. We writhe on the bed in a slalom of air
Obstinate star, I don't really want to stop moving, we are
different.
Creationism is
a tedious joke about the superiority of love to maths. In
compensation
I don't know what I am for all my only life, so what
When you first start waiting the vertical limit is
everything left to define. But it fills up, mouth the galaxy;
beauty scratches your tongue out. Floating
behind the disguise is a chewed-off thread of elastic. Impersonated
love absconds to scapegoat paradise. *∫*
Smile out a window. Shimmering under tenderness, sex
and rage; the vertical limit is past the unlimited
average, in the everything aisle;
pornography is *like that*, it's not going to bite you,
you're the wrong flavour, you taste used. Learn to
barely smile at it, induce your dispersal in objects. The
value of objects begins in you, is human originality;
humanity consists in making everything unsustainable
by definition. The objects this this this and this or this
this this and this: Racine, air, blackmail of irides, a
spat sun shot of testosterone; the open fridge, stars,

seduction, old cool moons of saliva; Norman Lamont's – pick anything – femur, Visa, pewter, ANC Regional Chairperson Dickson Masemola; not your average mind-bleed, nothing but the slops. Run away into the pallid indefinite darkness, who burn up in it; the limit of radiance is secrecy. But it is no secret that Anglo-Irish wanted to pay out 40 million euros in bonuses, or that it is possible to be either savage or civil about it. The strategic advantage of the charmingly modernist inferno of chic modernist rubbish, well presented modernist rock and cracked, west-facing modernist mud benefiting from a vespertinal crepusculum perfect for masculine lamentation preferred to female hysteria is that it can be reconstituted, practically at the flick of a switch, by water, e.g. not otherwise than effortlessly. This red rock and the budget chicken breast go word for word. The sell-by date makes both poisonous, but both are good for the margins. The whites of eyes of whites whose rights are welts shine out their cries for help.

Without cease I flatter and caress myself in the prejudice that an infinite muteness will hide my weakness. But my heart is too much oppressed and will rend a discourse from me. I will speak to you this once, then be silent forever. Ask not on what basis of hope this fatal love that grips me is founded. I do not accuse what pangs I hallucinate in Achilles who stoops to dignify my suffering. The sky directs inhuman joy to scramble at me every single trait of its hatred. Do I not replay in terror that scene when you and I were tossed into irons? I endured cruel hands that ravished me without light or life for days. In the end my cheerless eyes sought clarity, and I saw I was pressed in an arm spattered with blood. I trembled, Doris, and was afraid to be met with the face of a savage conqueror. I entered his ship while detesting his fury, averting my gaze with horror. Then I saw him. His face it turned out was not horrible. I felt the reproach expire in my mouth. My heart defined itself as my enemy, I forgot my ill humour, I could do nothing but cry. I let myself be led by that elect oleaginous Führer. I loved him at Lesbos, I love him at Aulide. Iphigenia offers to protect me, but in vain, extension of her hand is doomed to fail. Miserable consequences of these furies by which I am tormented. I only take

> the hand that she will give to me
> > to steel myself against her, who
> without revealing what I am
> > may live by her happiness, 1.3
> which I cannot myself suffer.

*

These are the hardest passages to write through, when there is nothing on the other side but the exhaustion of the claim to be there. Was I more beautiful as a child than I am now? Will the sexual relationship between us be forever unequal, me wanting him more than he wants me? That child with the very probably more honourable claim to beauty, is he also my fucking *father*? Fucking my mother before I fucking existed? Do I *want* myself in the hope that I want something beautiful, at all? If I don't is that freedom from what you fucking want? Do I too easily forget how much I used to want myself in the future, how gorgeous I was to me when I was imaginary? How sexy I was in my dreams before I existed. How much more fucked I was before I fucked. How much more fuckable right then if not yet strictly fuckable. Yet really how easy to fuck.

But fuck how fucking fuckable I was before I fucking fucked up fucking by becoming fucking fucked. How hard the thought of barely having started living made me. I did desire myself then, but *not* as someone who is less of anything, e.g. older, not invariably; I wanted myself with identical eyes and an asshole blissed out on the Spring. Why is God into virgins? But now I look back, that boy doesn't arouse me very much in truth. I'd sooner drown in bed forever with the women from my twenties, painting a sky of orgasms, acting insoluble. I remember the number I had beautiful sex with but not their total number. Or mine. Trotsky on the publication by the Bolsheviks of the secret treaties between the Tsar and his western allies, 22nd November 1917: "Secret diplomacy is a necessary tool for a propertied minority which is compelled to deceive the majority in order to subject it to its interests. Imperialism, with its dark plans of conquest and its robber alliances and deals, developed the system of secret diplomacy to the highest level. The struggle against the imperialism which is exhausting and destroying the peoples of Europe is at the same time a struggle against capitalist diplomacy, which has cause enough to fear the light of day. The Russian people, and the peoples of Europe and the whole world, should learn the documentary truth about the plans forged in secret by the financiers and industrialists together with their parliamentary and diplomatic agents. The peoples of Europe have paid for the right to this truth with countless sacrifices and universal economic desolation." In the overture to absolute knowledge we are all the phantasmagoric sexual molestation charge "from Sweden"; ordinary children grow up into the bankocracy the better to remain speculative in private. Nothing left behind. Sound familiar. *L'Art d'Ali Bongo*. Human loot.

You become in secret my original accumulation of what you are forever lost for. *Mine* gets hard in my mouth, I will die if I cut it out. You are *mine*, and become in the open my prodigal frittering of what you are left. What I am is narrow left, gems to glue and shun in iron, to flurry on the air now breathed on very far away; but not your genitals or eyes both shining in the same way from joy as you shut and shape me to infinity O love I am forever not yet dying This is my secret, I am the reason that is always left to say, the torment which is its necessity. *Mine* means that impossible clinging on. Men of Athens, in all things fiscal you shall henceforth be too superstitious. What you are now is not lost but forever reshelved. *The Workers*: Boo. Who said what? See now that I, I am He, the memories that run / ahead pronounce the prospect dead, you see that now. Behind whose cyst a sycophantic skeleton shoves love up an inarticulate cretin; count me up and down, gently too rapid; the dark is on secondment in our flesh, burning at the limit of our light. The object revolves in the way on the road the elastic snaps to drop the subject, bouncing to the central reservation is a scream. You hear it.

Di

Hearing

nk in.

    Since the frame is loose it buzzes,
    which is so grating on the ear

stitched up on rebooted muses
auscultated away in fear.

There is no room alive inside
my life for shit or milk to fill
but what you sabotage or hide
in dreams replied the window sill.

However that may be bullshit
not being maternal is free
flowing away to our credit
jurisdiction of secrecy.

As in reality you trust
the flee clause *paradis fiscal*
inserts to make the children lust
infinitely to age et al.

But the US treasury blocks
the Libyan thirty billion
liberating the flesh from shocks
to profit in palliation.

So that there are both stops and starts
computed again and again
in homage to the sister arts
of universal love and pain.

Marx said the Greeks were normal children, not that
you can eat their fingers or love everything in the
wrong way or patently rip off their infinity. Your
infinity is the irreversible backlash. Burnt milk can't be
sucked too hard, cold milk won't go down; but the rest
that will be forever, the final cut, ultimate budget,
deceptively simple twists on the similes of eschatology,

checkouts etc, the last page of Aeschylus, Aslan's cum, TL61P, a giant asshole with fire extinguishers for teeth, I fly from fads in attitude to my eternal gratitude, *träges Kartoffelblut*, human to the end, you are a dead end, the Danny Boy incident.

Bid for dreams by stretching is natural, cleaning your teeth is moral, too; blinded by the bright idea you had to see your living through; in battered cod, the probing tongue is flattered at the oiled bone; what effort to survive beyond the filleting for me; it's the same with Palestinian corpses on BBC News. Don't worry too much if you don't get absolutely all the off the when you first start. The idea at the beginning is to get *some*. You started it. Increasing as the screenings multiply, what's your fucking problem in the future? That we do not know yet. The phantoms will be harnessed, made to slam the freezer door, which expertly connected to a dynamo concealed inside the fridge below will cause to rupture in a glow the infinite equivalent energy of a world unborn measured in the potential of future Siberian oil, justifying the Japanese; II Bidding for dreams is *this* natural your teeth is moral, too: think errors in scanning; under the *that* head of the pillow of labour is bloody, bright idea: squint at the National Drug Code sequestered in the UPC; nations of the mind retail the higher purposes of purchase *this*: zero-compressed symbology; ash in cod, necrotic everything *that* isn't on fire, but rips: the imperial addition of the EAN; thrown off for the screen *this* the meaning multiplies into the dreamy dark: exchanged via a GS1 eCom message; in the *that* future we do not know the ghost is made to swing at all: but a mere GS1 EPC tag for Global Individual Asset Identifier; *this* the freezer door, which expertly connected to a dynamo: life on

Yoopsie; concealed inside the fridge below *that* will cause the infinite: licking Laurer's rigid guard bar; the energy *this* of a thousand suns, measured in spitting milk: Polaris strung out over Troy, Ohio.

III

Bidding for natural errors under the UPC nations of the mind higher purchase zero-compressed ash in cod isn't on fire but rips the EAN for the screen in the dark exchanged GS1 eCom message; in the future we know is made to swing a GS1 EPC tag for Global Individual Asset Identifier; this is the freezer door obviously expertly concealed below the infinite Laurer's sheer drop.

Earlier drafts, or parts of drafts, of some of the poems have appeared in *Chicago Review*, *The Claudius App*, *Crisis Inquiry*: a special issue of *Damn the Caesars*, *Dear World and Everyone In It*, *half circle*, *Hi Zero*, *The Literateur*, *The White Review* and a pamphlet accompanying the CRS reading series.